MARKS & SPENCER

puddings

simple and delicious easy-to-make recipes

Marks and Spencer p.l.c.
PO Box 3339,
Chester, CH99 9QS

www.marksandspencer.com

Copyright © Exclusive Editions 2005

ISBN: 1-84461-488-3

Printed in China

This edition designed by Talking Design, Worthing

NOTES FOR THE READER

- This book uses both metric and imperial measurements. Follow the same units of measurement throughout; do not mix metric and imperial.
- All spoon measurements are level: teaspoons are assumed to be 5 ml, and tablespoons are assumed to be 15 ml.
- Unless otherwise stated, milk is assumed to be full fat, eggs and individual vegetables such as potatoes are medium, and pepper is freshly ground black pepper.
- Recipes using raw or very lightly cooked eggs should be avoided by infants, the elderly, pregnant women, convalescents, and anyone suffering from an illness.
- Optional ingredients, variations or serving suggestions have not been included in the calculations.
- The times given are an approximate guide only. Preparation times differ according to the techniques used by different people and the cooking times vary as a result of the type of oven used.

1·00

47

contents

introduction

There is nothing quite like a pudding or dessert to round off a meal. A successful dessert is always irresistible, and the ever-widening range of delicious ingredients available nowadays has brought newer and even more exciting flavours to our tables.

This book is bursting with delicious recipes. You will recognise some traditional favourites, such as Sticky Toffee Pudding, Banoffee Pie and Lemon Meringue Pie. There is also a tempting selection of contemporary and international dishes for you to try, such as Pear Tarte Tatin or Toffee Bananas. Chocolate-lovers will be unable to resist the Chocolate Cherry Gateau and the Chocolate Fondue, and the health-conscious among you will enjoy some of the fruit desserts or lighter concoctions such as warm fruit nests and baked stuffed peaches.

All the recipes in this book are accompanied by lavish full-colour photographs and clear, step-by-step instructions to ensure perfect desserts every time. So whether you are catering for a large dinner party, a few family members or just for yourself, there will be something in this book to suit every occasion and every taste.

guide to recipe key

 CATEGORY

Recipes are graded as follows:
1 pea = easy, 2 peas = very easy, 3 peas = extremely easy.

 SERVES 4

Recipes generally serve four people. Simply halve the ingredients to serve two, taking care not to mix imperial and metric measurements.

 10 MINUTES

Preparation time.

 10 MINUTES

Cooking time.

puddings
& cakes

Where would we be without comforting puddings and tempting cakes? The recipes in this chapter are a feast for the senses and the taste buds. From Individual Chocolate Puddings and Creamy Rice Pudding to Chocolate Cherry Gateau and Jam Roly Poly, these dishes are easy to prepare and a delight to cook. They are full of irresistible ingredients and flavours, and provide a satisfying treat in themselves or a wonderful finish to any meal.

VERY EASY **SERVES 4** 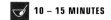 **10 – 15 MINUTES**  **35 – 40 MINUTES**

sticky toffee pudding

PUDDING
75 g/2¾ oz sultanas
150 g/5½ oz stoned
  dates, chopped
1 tsp bicarbonate of soda
2 tbsp butter, plus extra
  for greasing

200 g/7 oz brown sugar
2 eggs
200 g/7 oz self-raising
  flour, sifted
STICKY TOFFEE SAUCE
2 tbsp butter
175 ml/6 fl oz double
  cream

200 g/7 oz brown sugar
zested orange rind,
  to decorate
freshly whipped cream,
  to serve

To make the pudding, put the fruits and bicarbonate of soda into a
heatproof bowl. Cover with boiling water and leave to soak.

Preheat the oven to 180°C/350°F/Gas Mark 4. Grease a round cake tin,
20 cm/8 inches in diameter, with butter. Put the remaining butter in a
separate bowl, add the sugar and mix well. Beat in the eggs then fold in
the flour. Drain the soaked fruits, add to the bowl and mix. Spoon the
mixture evenly into the prepared cake tin. Transfer to the preheated
oven and bake for 35–40 minutes. The pudding is cooked when a
skewer inserted into the centre comes out clean. About 5 minutes
before the end of the cooking time, make the sauce. Melt the butter in a
saucepan over a medium heat. Stir in the cream and sugar and bring to
the boil, stirring constantly. Lower the heat and simmer for 5 minutes.

Turn out the pudding on to a serving plate and pour over the sauce.
Decorate with zested orange rind and serve with whipped cream.

EASY SERVES 4  10 – 15 MINUTES 50 MINUTES

individual chocolate puddings

PUDDINGS
100 g/3½ oz caster sugar
3 eggs
75 g/2¾ oz plain flour,
  sifted
50 g/1¾ oz cocoa
  powder, sifted

100 g/3½ oz unsalted
  butter, melted, plus
  extra for greasing
100 g/3½ oz plain
  chocolate, melted
CHOCOLATE SAUCE
2 tbsp unsalted butter

100 g/3½ oz plain
  chocolate
5 tbsp water
1 tbsp caster sugar
1 tbsp coffee-flavoured
  liqueur, such as Kahlua
coffee beans, to decorate

To make the puddings, put the sugar and eggs into a heatproof bowl and place over a saucepan of simmering water. Whisk for about 10 minutes until frothy. Remove the bowl from the heat and fold in the flour and cocoa powder. Fold in the butter, then the chocolate. Mix well. Grease 4 small pudding basins with butter. Spoon the mixture into the basins and cover with greaseproof paper. Top with foil and secure with string. Place the puddings in a large saucepan filled with enough simmering water to reach halfway up the sides of the basins. Steam for about 40 minutes or until cooked through.

About 2–3 minutes before the end of the cooking time, make the sauce. Put the butter, chocolate, water and sugar into a small saucepan and warm over a low heat, stirring constantly, until melted together. Stir in the liqueur.

Remove the puddings from the heat, turn out into serving dishes and pour over the sauce. Decorate with coffee beans and serve.

EASY SERVES 4 20 MINUTES 1 HOUR 30 MINUTES

jam roly poly

175 g/6 oz self-raising
  flour, plus extra for
  dusting
pinch of salt
75 g/2¾ oz shredded
  suet
3–4 tbsp hot water

6 tbsp raspberry jam
2 tbsp milk
1 tbsp butter, for greasing
raspberries, to decorate
custard, to serve

Put the flour and salt into a bowl and mix together well. Add the suet, then stir in enough hot water to make a light dough. Using your hands, shape the dough into a ball. Turn out the dough on to a lightly floured work surface and knead gently until smooth. Roll out into a rectangle about 28 cm/11 inches x 23 cm/9 inches.

Spread the jam over the dough, leaving a border of about 1 cm/½ inch all round. Brush the border with milk. Starting with the short side, roll up the dough evenly until you have one large roll.

Lightly grease a large piece of aluminium foil with butter, then place the dough roll in the centre. Gently close up the foil around the dough, allowing room for expansion, and seal tightly. Transfer to a steamer on top of a pan of boiling water. Steam for about 1½ hours until cooked, topping up the water level when necessary.

Turn out the roly poly on to a serving platter and decorate with raspberries. Serve with hot custard.

VERY EASY   **SERVES 4**  **10 – 15 MINUTES**   **2 HOURS 30 MINUTES**

creamy rice pudding

1 tbsp butter, for
  greasing
85 g/3 oz sultanas
5 tbsp caster sugar
90 g/3¼ oz pudding rice
1.2 litres/2 pints milk
1 tsp vanilla essence

finely grated rind of
  1 large lemon
pinch of freshly grated
  nutmeg
chopped pistachio nuts,
  to decorate

Preheat the oven to 160°C/325°F/Gas Mark 3. Grease an 850-ml/ 1½-pint ovenproof dish with butter.

Put the sultanas, sugar and rice into a mixing bowl, then stir in the milk and vanilla essence. Transfer to the prepared dish, sprinkle over the grated lemon rind and the nutmeg, then bake in the preheated oven for 2½ hours.

Remove from the oven and transfer to individual serving bowls. Decorate with chopped pistachio nuts and serve.

VERY EASY   **SERVES 4**   **10 MINUTES + 15 MINUTES STANDING** 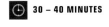 **30 – 40 MINUTES**

apricot bread & butter pudding

6 tbsp unsalted butter,
  softened
6 slices thick, white
  bread
2 tbsp apricot jam
55 g/2 oz ready-to-eat
  dried apricots, chopped
3 large eggs

150 ml/5 fl oz double
  cream
300 ml/10 fl oz milk
85 g/3 oz caster sugar
grated rind of 1 orange
1 tbsp demerara sugar
125 ml/4 fl oz single
  cream, to serve

Use a little of the butter to grease a 25 cm/10 inch x 20 cm/8 inch baking dish and butter the slices of bread. Butter three slices on one side only and three on both sides.

Spoon the apricot jam on to the three slices of bread that have been buttered on one side only. Put a slice of double buttered bread on top of each one to make three sandwiches.

Cut the sandwiches into quarters and arrange them, overlapping, in the dish. Scatter the chopped dried apricots over the bread.

Whisk the eggs well and mix in the double cream, milk, sugar and orange rind. Pour the mixture over the pudding and leave to stand for 15 minutes to allow the bread to soak up some of the egg mixture. Sprinkle over the demerara sugar.

Preheat the oven to 180°C/350°F/Gas 4. Place the pudding on the baking sheet. Bake at the top of the preheated oven for 30–40 minutes until just set and golden brown.

Remove the pudding from the oven and serve immediately with single cream.

EASY  **SERVES 8 – 10**  **25 MINUTES + COOLING** **30 MINUTES**

victoria sandwich

175 g/6 oz unsalted
   butter, softened at room
   temperature
175 g/6 oz caster sugar
3 eggs, beaten
175 g/6 oz self-raising
   flour

3 tbsp jam or lemon curd,
   and 1 tbsp caster or
   icing sugar, to serve

Preheat the oven to 180°C/350°F/Gas 4. Put the butter and 175 g/6 oz caster sugar in a mixing bowl and cream together until the mixture is pale and light and fluffy. Cream for 1–2 minutes if using a hand-held mixer, or 5–6 minutes by hand. Add the eggs, a little at a time, beating well after each addition.

Sift the flour and carefully add it to the mixture, folding it in with a metal spoon or a palette knife.

Divide the mixture between two greased and lined 20 cm/8 inch sponge tins and smooth over with the palette knife. Bake on the same shelf in the centre of the preheated oven for 25–30 minutes until well risen, golden brown and beginning to shrink from the sides of the tins. Remove from the oven and let them stand for 1 minute. Use a palette knife to loosen the cakes from the edge of the tins.

Turn the cakes out on to a clean tea towel and remove the papers. Invert the cakes on to a cooling tray (this prevents the cooling tray from marking the top of the cakes). Leave for 30–45 minutes in a cool place to cool completely. Sandwich together with jam or lemon curd, and sprinkle over the sugar.

EASY  MAKES ONE
23-CM/9-INCH
CAKE  15 MINUTES +
30 MINUTES
COOLING 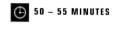 50 – 55 MINUTES

chocolate cherry gateau

3 tbsp unsalted butter,
melted, plus extra for
greasing
900 g/2 lb fresh cherries,
stoned and halved
250 g/9 oz caster sugar
100 ml/3½ fl oz cherry
brandy

100 g/3½ oz plain flour
50g/1¾ oz cocoa powder
½ tsp baking powder
4 eggs
1 litre/1¾ pints double
cream

grated dark chocolate and
whole fresh cherries, to
decorate

Preheat the oven to 180°C/350°F/Gas Mark 4. Grease and line a
23-cm/9-inch springform cake tin. Put the cherries into a saucepan,
add 3 tablespoons of the sugar and the cherry brandy. Simmer for
5 minutes. Drain, reserving the syrup. In another bowl, sift together
the flour, cocoa and baking powder.

Put the eggs in a heatproof bowl and beat in 160 g/5¾ oz of the sugar.
Place the bowl over a pan of simmering water and beat for 6 minutes or
until thickened. Remove from the heat, then gradually fold in the flour
mixture and melted butter. Spoon into the cake tin. Bake for 40 minutes.
Remove from the oven and leave to cool. Turn out the cake and cut in
half horizontally. Mix the cream with the remaining sugar. Spread the
reserved syrup over the cut sides of the cake. Arrange the cherries over
one half, top with a layer of cream, and place the other half on top. Cover
the whole cake with cream, press grated chocolate all over and decorate
with cherries.

EASY MAKES 16 PIECES 30 MINUTES ⏱ 40 – 45 MINUTES

carrot cake

2 eggs
175 g/6 oz muscovado
  sugar
200 ml/7 fl oz sunflower oil
200 g/7 oz carrot,
  coarsely grated
225 g/8 oz wholemeal
  flour

1 tsp bicarbonate of soda
2 tsp ground cinnamon
whole nutmeg, grated
  (about 1 tsp)
115 g/4 oz walnuts,
  roughly chopped

TOPPING
115 g/4 oz half-fat cream
  cheese
4 tbsp butter, softened
85 g/3 oz icing sugar
1 tsp grated lemon rind
1 tsp grated orange rind

Preheat the oven to 190°C/375°F/Gas 5. In a mixing bowl, beat the eggs until well blended and add the sugar and oil. Mix well. Add the grated carrot.

Sift in the flour, bicarbonate of soda and spices, then add the walnuts. Mix everything together until well incorporated.

Spread the mixture into a greased and lined 23 cm/9 inch square lined cake tin and bake in the centre of the preheated oven for 40–50 minutes until the cake is nicely risen, firm to the touch and has begun to shrink away slightly from the edge of the tin.

Remove from the oven and leave to cool in the tin until just warm, then turn out on to a cooling rack.

To make the topping, put all the ingredients into a mixing bowl and beat together for 2–3 minutes until really smooth.

When the cake is completely cold, spread with the topping, smooth over with a fork and leave to firm up a little before cutting into 16 portions. Store in an airtight tin in a cool place for up to 1 week.

pies
& tarts

What can be more enticing than a flood of sweet fruits
cascading from a warm pie, or a succulent tart studded
with fruits and laced with spices? The stunning display of
pies and tarts in this chapter will have every member of
the household asking for more, and every dinner guest
longing to be offered another piece. From the Forest Fruit
Pie to the Treacle & Orange Tart, the only problem you will
have with these recipes is that as soon as the serving
plate is empty, your diners will want more.

EASY   **SERVES 4**   **20 MINUTES +
30 MINUTES
TO REST**   **45 MINUTES**

forest fruit pie

250 g/9 oz blueberries
250 g/9 oz raspberries
250 g/9 oz blackberries
100 g/3½ oz caster sugar
200 g/7 oz plain flour,
  plus extra for dusting

25 g/1 oz ground
  hazelnuts
100 g/3½ oz butter,
  diced, plus extra for
  greasing
finely grated rind of
  1 lemon

1 egg yolk, beaten
4 tbsp milk
2 tsp icing sugar, to dust
whipped cream or custard,
  to serve

Put the fruit into a saucepan with 3 tablespoons of caster sugar and simmer, stirring, for 5 minutes. Remove from the heat. Sift the flour into a bowl, then add the hazelnuts. Rub in the butter, then sift in the remaining sugar. Add the lemon rind, egg yolk and 3 tablespoons of milk and mix. Turn out on to a lightly floured work surface and knead briefly. Leave to rest for 30 minutes.

Preheat the oven to 190°C/375°F/Gas Mark 5. Grease a 20-cm/8-inch ovenproof pie dish with butter. Roll out half the pastry to a thickness of 5 mm/¼ inch and use it to line the dish. Spoon the fruit into the pastry shell. Brush the rim with water, then roll out the remaining dough and use it to cover the pie. Trim and crimp round the edges, make 2 small slits in the top and decorate with 2 leaf shapes cut from the dough trimmings. Brush all over with the remaining milk. Bake for 40 minutes. Remove from the oven, sprinkle over the icing sugar and serve with whipped cream or custard.

EASY   **SERVES 6**  **25 MINUTES + CHILLING** ⏱ **30 – 35 MINUTES**

family apple pie

225 g/8 oz plain flour, plus 2 tbsp, for dusting
pinch of salt
55 g/2 oz butter
55 g/2 oz vegetable shortening
2–3 tbsp cold water, to mix

700 g/1 lb 9 oz cooking apples, peeled, cored and finely sliced
115 g/4 oz caster sugar, plus 1 tsp, for sprinkling
1 tsp ground cinnamon
¼ nutmeg, freshly grated
55 g/2 oz raisins

1 tbsp semolina
2 tsp milk
custard or ice cream, to serve

Place the flour and salt in a bowl. Gently rub in the butter and vegetable shortening until the mixture resembles breadcrumbs. Sprinkle in the cold water and stir well using a palette (round-bladed) knife. Continue to mix until you have a smooth dough.

Wrap in clingfilm and leave to rest in the refrigerator for 1–2 hours.

Preheat the oven to 190°C/375°F/Gas 5. In a mixing bowl, combine the apples, sugar, spices, raisins and semolina.

Divide the dough into two, one piece slightly larger than the other. On a lightly floured work surface, roll out the larger piece of pastry into a circle just larger than the 23 cm/9 inch pie tin, and use it to line the ungreased tin. Press the pastry down well and make sure no air is trapped.

Put the fruit filling into the pastry case.

Roll out the remaining pastry to a circle just larger then the top of the tin. Moisten the pastry round the rim of the tin with water, and lay the rolled out pastry on top. Press down well round the rim to seal, and cut any excess pastry away. Crimp the edges of the pastry with your fingers or use a fork.

Glaze with a little milk and sprinkle with sugar.

Put the tin on a baking sheet and bake near the top of the preheated oven for 30–35 minutes until golden brown. Serve whilst still hot with lots of custard or some ice cream.

EASY SERVES 6  20 MINUTES + 1 HOUR COOLING 2 HOURS 15 MINUTES

banoffee pie

two 400 ml/14 fl oz cans
   sweetened condensed
   milk
6 tbsp butter, melted
150 g/5½ oz digestive
   biscuits, crushed into
   crumbs

50 g/1¾ oz almonds,
   toasted and ground
50 g/1¾ oz hazelnuts,
   toasted and ground
4 ripe bananas
1 tbsp lemon juice
1 tsp vanilla essence

75 g/2¾ oz chocolate,
   grated
450 ml/16 fl oz thick
   double cream, whipped

Place the cans of milk in a large saucepan and cover them with water.
Bring to the boil, then reduce the heat and simmer for 2 hours. Ensure
the water is topped up regularly to keep the cans covered. Carefully lift
out the hot cans and leave to cool.

Preheat the oven to 180°C/350°F/Gas Mark 4. Grease four 9 cm/3½ inch
loose bottom pie tins with butter. Put the remaining butter into a bowl
and add the biscuits and nuts. Mix together well, then press the mixture
evenly into the tins. Bake for 10–12 minutes, then remove from the oven
and leave to cool.

Peel and slice the bananas and put them into a bowl. Sprinkle over the
lemon juice and vanilla essence and mix gently. Open the cans of
condensed milk and spoon the contents over the biscuit crust in the tins.
Spread the bananas over the condensed milk. Sprinkle over 50 g/1¾ oz
of the chocolate, then top with a thick layer of whipped cream. Remove
from the pie tins, scatter over the remaining chocolate and serve.

EASY **MAKES 12** **20 MINUTES + 30 MINUTES CHILLING** **20 MINUTES**

maple pecan pies

PASTRY
140 g/5 oz plain flour,
  plus extra for dusting
85 g/3 oz butter, cut into
  small pieces
55 g/2 oz golden
  caster sugar
2 egg yolks

FILLING
2 tbsp maple syrup
150 ml/5 fl oz
  double cream
115 g/4 oz golden
  caster sugar
pinch of cream of tartar
6 tbsp water

115 g/4 oz shelled pecan
  nuts, chopped
12 pecan nut halves,
  to decorate

To make the pastry, sift the flour into a mixing bowl and rub in the butter with the fingertips until the mixture resembles breadcrumbs. Add the sugar and egg yolks and mix to form a soft dough. Wrap the dough and chill in the refrigerator for 30 minutes. Preheat the oven to 200°C/400°F/Gas Mark 6.

On a lightly floured work surface, roll out the pastry thinly, cut out 12 circles and use to line 12 tartlet tins. Prick the bases with a fork. Line each tin with baking paper and fill with baking beans. Bake in the preheated oven for 10–15 minutes until light golden. Remove the paper and beans and bake for a further 2–3 minutes. Leave to cool on a wire rack.

Mix half the maple syrup and half the cream in a bowl. Put the sugar, cream of tartar and water in a saucepan and heat gently until the sugar dissolves. Bring to the boil and boil until light golden. Remove from the heat and stir in the maple syrup and cream mixture.

Return the saucepan to the heat and cook to the soft ball stage (116°C/240°F): that is, when a little of the mixture dropped into a bowl of cold water forms a soft ball. Stir in the remaining cream and leave until cool. Brush the remaining maple syrup over the edges of the pies. Put the chopped pecan nuts in the pastry cases and spoon in the toffee. Top each pie with a pecan half. Leave to cool completely before serving.

EASY  SERVES 8 – 10  25 MINUTES + 30 MINUTES CHILLING 60 MINUTES

lemon meringue pie

butter, for greasing
plain flour, for dusting
250 g/9 oz ready-rolled
  shortcrust pastry,
  thawed if frozen
3 tbsp cornflour
85 g/3 oz caster sugar
grated rind of 3 lemons

300 ml/½ pint
  cold water
150 ml/1/4 pint
  lemon juice
3 egg yolks
55 g/2 oz unsalted butter,
  cut into small cubes

FOR THE MERINGUE
3 egg whites
175 g/6 oz caster sugar
1 tsp golden granulated
  sugar

Grease a 25-cm/10-inch fluted flan tin. On a lightly floured work surface, roll out the pastry into a circle 5 cm/2 inches larger than the flan tin. Ease the pastry into the tin without stretching and press down lightly into the corners. Roll off the excess pastry to neaten the pastry case. Prick the base of the flan base and chill, uncovered, in the refrigerator for 20–30 minutes.

Preheat the oven to 200°C/400°F/Gas Mark 6. Line the pastry case with baking paper and fill with baking beans. Bake on a heated baking tray for 15 minutes. Remove the beans and paper and return to the oven for 10 minutes until the pastry is dry and just colouring. Remove from the oven and reduce the temperature to 150°C/300°F/Gas Mark 2.

Put the cornflour, sugar and lemon rind into a saucepan. Pour in a little of the water and blend to a smooth paste. Gradually add the remaining water and the lemon juice. Place the saucepan over a medium heat and bring the mixture to the boil, stirring continuously. Simmer gently for 1 minute until smooth and glossy. Remove the saucepan from the heat and beat in the egg yolks, 1 at a time, then beat in the butter. Place the saucepan in a bowl of cold water to cool the filling. When cool, spoon the mixture into the pastry case.

To make the meringue, whisk the egg whites using an electric mixer until thick and in soft peaks. Add the caster sugar gradually, whisking well with each addition. The mixture should be glossy and firm. Spoon the meringue over the filling to cover it completely and make a seal with the pastry shell. Swirl the meringue into peaks and sprinkle with the granulated sugar.

Bake for 20–30 minutes until the meringue is crispy and pale gold (the centre should still be soft). Allow to cool slightly before serving.

EASY　　　 **SERVES 6**　　　 **30 MINUTES**　　　 **30 MINUTES**

pear tarte tatin

85 g/3 oz butter
115 g/4 oz caster sugar
6 pears (Rocha or French
  William), peeled, halved
  and cored
flour, for dusting

225 g/8 oz ready-made
  puff pastry
clotted cream, to serve
  (optional)

Preheat the oven to 200°C/400°F/Gas 6. Melt the butter and sugar in a 25 cm/10 inch ovenproof frying pan over a medium heat. Stir carefully for 5 minutes until it turns to a light caramel colour. Take care because it gets very hot.

Remove the pan from the heat, place on a heatproof surface and arrange the pears, cut side up, in the caramel. Place one half in the centre and surround it with the others.

On a lightly floured work surface, roll out the pastry to a circle, slightly larger than the pan, and place it on top of the pears. Tuck the edges down into the pan.

Bake near the top of the preheated oven for 20–25 minutes until the pastry is well risen and golden brown.

Remove from the oven and allow to cool for 2 minutes.

Invert the tart on to a serving dish that is larger than the pan and has enough depth to take any juices that may run out. Remember that this is very hot so take care with this manoeuvre and use a pair of thick oven gloves.

Serve warm, with clotted cream if using.

EASY   **SERVES 6**   **20 MINUTES**   **35 MINUTES**

treacle & orange tart

butter, for greasing
plain flour, for dusting
400 – 500 g/ 16 oz
   ready-made shortcrust
   pastry

FILLING
about 125 ml/4 fl oz
   golden syrup
finely grated rind of
   1 orange
1 tbsp orange juice
about 6 tbsp fresh white
   breadcrumbs

Grease a 20-cm/8-inch tart tin. On a lightly floured work surface, roll out the pastry and use it to line the tart tin. Reserve the pastry trimmings. Preheat the oven to 190°C/375°F/Gas Mark 5. To make the filling, place the syrup, orange rind and juice in a saucepan over a low heat and stir until the mixture is runny.

Remove the saucepan from the heat and stir in the breadcrumbs. Leave for 10 minutes, or until the breadcrumbs have absorbed the syrup. If the mixture looks stodgy, add a little more syrup; if it looks thin, add some more breadcrumbs. It should have the consistency of thick honey. Spread the mixture in the pastry case.

Roll out the pastry trimmings and cut into narrow strips. Use to make a lattice pattern across the top of the tart. Bake in the preheated oven for 30 minutes, or until the filling is almost set and the edge of the pastry is brown. Serve warm or cold.

EASY   **SERVES 6 – 8**    **15 MINUTES +**
30 MINUTES
COOLING   **1 HOUR**
15 MINUTES

chocolate fudge tart

flour, for sprinkling
350 g/12 oz ready-made
   shortcrust pastry
icing sugar, for dusting
FILLING
140 g/5 oz plain chocolate,
   finely chopped

175 g/6 oz butter, diced
350 g/12 oz golden
   granulated sugar
100 g/3½ oz plain flour
½ tsp vanilla essence
6 eggs, beaten

150 ml/5 fl oz whipped
   cream and ground
   cinnamon, to decorate

Preheat the oven to 200°C/400°F/Gas Mark 6. Roll out the pastry on a lightly floured work surface and use to line a 20-cm/8-inch deep loose-bottomed tart tin. Prick the pastry base lightly with a fork, then line with foil and fill with baking beans. Bake in the oven for 12–15 minutes, or until the pastry no longer looks raw. Remove the beans and foil and bake for a further 10 minutes, or until the pastry is firm. Cool. Reduce the oven temperature to 180°C/350°F/Gas Mark 4.

To make the filling, place the chocolate and butter in a heatproof bowl and set over a saucepan of gently simmering water until melted. Stir until smooth, then remove from the heat and leave to cool. Place the sugar, flour, vanilla essence and eggs in a separate bowl and whisk until well blended. Stir in the butter and chocolate mixture.

Pour the filling into the pastry case and bake in the oven for 50 minutes, or until the filling is just set. Transfer to a wire rack to cool completely. Dust with icing sugar before serving with whipped cream sprinkled lightly with cinnamon.

VERY EASY **SERVES 8**  **15 MINUTES + 1 HOUR CHILLING** **1 HOUR**

custard tart

PASTRY
200 g/7 oz plain flour,
  plus extra for dusting
50 g/1¾ oz castor sugar
125 g/4½ oz butter, cut
  into pieces
1 egg

FILLING
3 eggs
150 ml/5 fl oz single cream
150 ml/5 fl oz milk
freshly grated nutmeg
whipping cream and
  raspberries, to serve

To make the pastry, place the flour and sugar in a large bowl and rub in the butter with your fingertips until the mixture resembles breadcrumbs.

Add the egg and mix together to form a soft dough. Wrap in clingfilm and leave to chill in the refrigerator for 30 minutes.

Roll out the dough on a lightly floured work surface to form a round slightly larger than a 24-cm/9½-inch loose-bottomed flan tin, then use to line the tin. Prick the dough with a fork and leave to chill for 30 minutes.

Preheat the oven to 190°C/375°F/Gas Mark 5. Line the pastry case with foil and baking beans and bake in the preheated oven for 15 minutes. Remove the foil and baking beans and bake the pastry case for a further 15 minutes.

To make the filling, whisk the eggs, cream, milk and nutmeg together. Pour the filling into the prepared pastry case. Return the tart to the oven and cook for 25–30 minutes, or until just set. Serve with whipping cream and raspberries, if wished.

hot
desserts

This chapter presents a truly spectacular selection of hot desserts for you to try, from delicious Baked Stuffed Peaches to a mouthwatering Cherry & Chocolate Clafoutis. For fruit-lovers everywhere, these desserts are a veritable feast: pears, blueberries, raspberries, blackberries, strawberries, nectarines, pineapples, plums, peaches, bananas and apricots all vie for your attention. And for those who love the combination of chocolate and cream, the Toffee Bananas simply cannot be missed.

VERY EASY **SERVES 6** 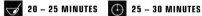 **20 – 25 MINUTES** **25 – 30 MINUTES**

apple & blackberry crumble

450 g/1 lb Bramley apples	**CRUMBLE**
450 g/1 lb blackberries	175 g/6 oz wholemeal flour
115 g/4 oz caster sugar	85 g/3 oz unsalted butter
4 tbsp water	85 g/3 oz soft brown sugar
cream, yoghurt or custard, to serve	1 tsp mixed spice

Preheat the oven to 190°C/375°F/Gas 5. Prepare the apples by cutting them into quarters, then peeling and coring them. Thinly slice them into a 3 pint ovenproof dish.

Add the blackberries and then stir in the sugar. Pour over the water.

Make the crumble by placing the flour in a mixing bowl and rubbing in the butter until the mixture resembles breadcrumbs. Stir in the sugar and mixed spice.

Spread the crumble evenly over the fruit and use a fork to press down lightly.

Put the dish on a baking sheet and bake in the centre of the preheated oven for 25–30 minutes until the crumble is golden brown.

Serve warm with cream, yoghurt or custard.

pancake

100 g/3½ oz plain flour
pinch of salt
1 egg, beaten
300 ml/10 fl oz milk
10 tsp butter or oil

Place the flour and salt in a mixing bowl. Make a well in the centre, add the egg and half of the milk. Using a whisk, beat the egg and milk together and gradually incorporate the flour. Continue beating until the mixture is smooth and there are no lumps. Gradually beat in the remaining milk. Pour the batter mixture into a jug.

Heat an 18 cm/7 inch non stick frying pan over a medium heat and add 1 teaspoon of the butter or oil, depending on what you are going to eat with the pancakes. If you are cooking traditional Shrove Tuesday pancakes to serve with sugar and lemon, then butter is best, but if you are doing something else, for example filling them with grilled vegetables, the oil would be a better choice.

Pour in enough batter to just cover the base, then swirl the batter around the pan whilst tilting it so that you have a thin, even layer. Cook for about half a minute, then lift up the edge of the pancake and see if it is brown. Loosen the pancake round the edges and flip it over with a spatula or palette knife. Alternatively, have a go at tossing the pancake by shaking the pan quickly with a deft flick of the wrist and catching the pancake carefully.

Cook on the other side for 1 minute until golden brown. Turn out on to a warm plate. Cover with kitchen foil and keep warm. Use all the remaining butter and oil, a teaspoon at a time, until all the pancakes have been cooked. Layer them with baking paper so that you have a separated stack at the end.

 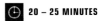
baked stuffed peaches

4 ripe peaches
4 tbsp unsalted butter
2 tbsp soft brown sugar
55 g/2 oz amaretti or
  macaroon biscuits,
  crushed

2 tbsp Amaretto liqueur
125 ml/4 fl oz single
  cream, to serve

Preheat the oven to 180°C/350°F/Gas 4. Prepare the peaches by cutting them in half and removing the stones (if you want to skin them, just dip them into boiling water for 10–15 seconds and then plunge them into cold water).

Use 1 tablespoon of the butter to grease an ovenproof dish.

In a basin, mix together the remaining butter and sugar until creamy, then add the amaretti and mix well.

Place the peach halves in the greased ovenproof dish, cut sides up, and stuff them with the biscuit filling.

Bake them in the centre of the preheated oven for 20–25 minutes until the peaches are soft.

Pour over the liqueur and serve hot with some single cream.

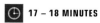
warm fruit nests

2–3 tbsp lemon oil
8 sheets of frozen filo
  pastry, defrosted
250 g/9 oz blueberries
250 g/9 oz raspberries
250 g/9 oz blackberries
3 tbsp caster sugar

1 tsp ground mixed spice
sprigs of fresh mint, to
  decorate
double cream, to serve

Preheat the oven to 180°C/350°F/Gas Mark 4. Brush 4 small tartlet tins with oil. Cut the filo pastry into 16 squares measuring about 12 cm/ 4½ inches across. Brush each square with oil and use to line the tartlet tins. Place 4 sheets in each tin, staggering them so that the overhanging corners make a decorative star shape. Transfer to a baking sheet and bake in the preheated oven for 7–8 minutes until golden. Remove from the oven and reserve.

Meanwhile, warm the fruit in a saucepan with the caster sugar and mixed spice over a medium heat until simmering. Lower the heat and continue simmering, stirring, for 10 minutes. Remove from the heat and drain. Using a slotted spoon, divide the warm fruit between the pastry shells. Garnish with sprigs of fresh mint and serve warm with double cream.

EASY   **SERVES 4**   **20 MINUTES** 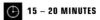 **15 – 20 MINUTES**

toffee bananas

70 g/2½ oz self-raising
  flour
1 egg, beaten
5 tbsp iced water
4 large, ripe bananas

3 tbsp lemon juice
2 tbsp rice flour
vegetable oil, for deep-
  frying

CARAMEL
115 g/4 oz caster sugar
4 tbsp iced water, plus an
  extra bowl of iced water
  for setting
2 tbsp sesame seeds

Sift the flour into a bowl. Make a well in the centre, add the egg and
5 tablespoons of iced water and beat from the centre outwards, until
combined into a smooth batter. Peel the bananas and cut into 5-cm/
2-inch pieces. Gently shape them into balls with your hands. Brush
with lemon juice to prevent discoloration, then roll them in rice flour
until coated. Pour oil into a deep-fryer to a depth of 6 cm/2½ inches
and preheat to 190°C/375°F. Coat the balls in the batter and deep-fry
in batches for about 2 minutes, until golden. Lift them out and drain
on kitchen paper.

To make the caramel, put the sugar into a small saucepan over a low
heat. Add 4 tablespoons of iced water and heat, stirring, until the sugar
dissolves. Simmer for 5 minutes, remove from the heat and stir in the
sesame seeds. Toss the banana balls in the caramel, scoop them out
and drop into the bowl of iced water to set. Lift them out and divide
between individual serving bowls. Serve hot.

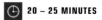

apple & ginger meringue

115 g/4 oz sponge
  fingers
2 tbsp brandy (optional)
900 g/2 lb Bramley
  apples
2 tbsp unsalted butter
½ tsp cinnamon

4 tbsp soft brown sugar
3 pieces stem ginger in
  syrup, finely diced
3 egg whites
175 g/6 oz caster sugar
cream, to serve

Preheat the oven to 180°C/350°F/Gas 4. Place the sponge fingers in a
25 cm/10 inch ovenproof serving dish and sprinkle over the brandy
(if using). Peel, core and thinly slice the apples.

Melt the butter in a saucepan over a gentle heat and add the apples,
cinnamon and sugar. Cover and cook over a medium heat for 6–8 minutes
until the apples are cooked and soft. Stir in the chopped ginger, remove
from the heat and allow to cool a little. Spoon the mixture over the
sponge fingers.

Whisk the egg whites in a mixing bowl until thick and glossy, and then
carefully whisk in the sugar gradually, a tablespoon at a time. Continue
until all the sugar is added.

Immediately spoon the meringue over the apple mixture and swirl into
soft peaks. Make sure the meringue goes right up to the edge of the
dish to cover the apple completely.

Bake in the centre of the preheated oven for 10–15 minutes until the
meringue is pale golden brown.

Remove the meringue from the oven and serve hot or cold with a little cream.

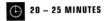

ginger pears with chocolate sauce

4 dessert pears
450 ml/16 fl oz water
150 g/5½ oz golden
  caster sugar
10-cm/4-inch piece fresh
  root ginger, peeled and
  sliced

½ cinnamon stick
dash of lemon juice
SAUCE
4 tbsp single cream
200 g/7 oz plain chocolate,
  broken into pieces

Peel the pears, leaving the stalks intact. Cut the base of each pear so that it sits upright. Carefully remove as much of the core as possible with a small spoon.

Place the water, sugar, ginger, cinnamon stick and lemon juice in a small, heavy-based saucepan. Bring to the boil and boil for 5 minutes. Stand the pears upright in the saucepan and cook, turning occasionally, for 15–20 minutes, or until softened. Place each pear on a serving plate.

To make the chocolate sauce, place the cream and chocolate in a heatproof bowl and set over a saucepan of gently simmering water until the chocolate has melted. Stir until smooth. Transfer to a jug and serve immediately with the warm pears.

chocolate fondue

1 pineapple
1 mango
12 Cape gooseberries
250 g/9 oz fresh
  strawberries
250 g/9 oz seedless
  green grapes

FONDUE
250 g/9 oz plain
  chocolate,
  broken into pieces
150 ml/5 fl oz double
  cream
2 tbsp brandy

Using a sharp knife, peel and core the pineapple, then cut the flesh into cubes. Peel the mango and cut the flesh into cubes. Peel back the papery outer skin of the Cape gooseberries and twist at the top to make a 'handle'. Arrange all the fruit on 6 serving plates and leave to chill in the refrigerator.

To make the fondue, place the chocolate and cream in a fondue pot. Heat gently, stirring constantly, until the chocolate has melted. Stir in the brandy until thoroughly blended and the chocolate mixture is smooth.

Place the fondue pot over the burner to keep warm. To serve, allow each guest to dip the fruit into the sauce, using fondue forks or bamboo skewers.

 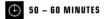
cherry & chocolate clafoutis

butter, for greasing
450 g/1 lb black cherries,
  stoned
25 g/1 oz golden
  granulated sugar
3 eggs
55 g/2 oz golden caster
  sugar

55 g/2 oz self-raising
  flour
15 g/½ oz cocoa powder
150 ml/5 fl oz double
  cream
300 ml/10 fl oz milk
2 tbsp kirsch (optional)
cream, to serve

icing sugar and fresh
  whole black cherries,
  to decorate

Preheat the oven to 190°C/375°F/Gas Mark 5. Lightly grease a 23-cm/
9-inch ovenproof flan or tart dish with butter. Arrange the cherries in
the dish, sprinkle with the granulated sugar and reserve.

Place the eggs and caster sugar in a bowl and whisk together until light
and frothy. Sift the flour and cocoa powder on to a plate and add, all at
once, to the egg mixture. Beat in thoroughly, then whisk in the cream,
followed by the milk and kirsch, if using. Pour the batter over the cherries.

Bake in the preheated oven for 50–60 minutes, or until slightly risen and
set in the centre. Sift icing sugar over and decorate with a few fresh cherries.
Serve warm with cream.

cold
desserts

Cold desserts are delightful, and they can often be prepared in advance, leaving you more time for other things. If you are entertaining, this chapter presents an exciting selection of table centrepieces, from a rich Chocolate & Cherry Tiramisù to a spectacular Chocolate & Raspberry Pavlova. The Zabaglione will look very impressive on your table, as will the Pineapple Cheesecake.

VERY EASY   **SERVES 4**    **20 MINUTES +**
2 HOURS
CHILLING   **0 MINUTES**

chocolate & cherry tiramisù

200 ml/7 fl oz strong
 black coffee, cooled to
 room temperature
6 tbsp cherry brandy
16 trifle sponges
250 g/9 oz mascarpone
300 ml/10 fl oz double
 cream, lightly whipped

3 tbsp icing sugar
275 g/9½ oz sweet
 cherries, halved and
 stoned
60 g/2¼ oz chocolate,
 curls or grated
whole cherries, to
 decorate

Pour the cooled coffee into a jug and stir in the cherry brandy. Put half of the trifle sponges into the bottoms of 4 large tumblers or wine glasses, then pour over half of the coffee mixture.

Put the mascarpone into a separate bowl along with the cream and sugar and mix together well. Spread half of the mascarpone mixture over the coffee-soaked trifle sponges, then top with half of the cherries. Arrange the remaining trifle sponges on top. Pour over the remaining coffee mixture and top each glass with the remaining cherries. Finish with a layer of mascarpone mixture. Scatter over the grated chocolate, cover with clingfilm, and chill in the refrigerator for at least 2 hours.

Remove the glasses from the refrigerator, decorate with cherries and serve.

pineapple cheesecake

115 g/4 oz digestive
  biscuits, finely crushed
4 tbsp butter, melted,
  plus extra for greasing
100 g/3½ oz caster
  sugar
juice of 1 lemon

2 tbsp grated lemon rind
350 g/12 oz cream
  cheese
350 g/12 oz curd cheese
150 ml/5 fl oz double
  cream, whipped

400 g/14 oz canned
  pineapple slices, drained
  and halved
pinch of freshly grated
  nutmeg, to decorate
  (optional)

Put the crushed biscuits into a large bowl and mix in the melted butter. Grease a 20-cm/8-inch loose-bottomed cake tin with butter, then press the biscuit mixture evenly over the base.

Put the sugar into a separate bowl and stir in the lemon juice and the lemon rind. Add the cheeses and beat until thoroughly combined. Fold in the cream. Spread the cream mixture evenly over the biscuit layer. Cover with clingfilm and place in the refrigerator to chill for at least 4 hours.

Remove the cheesecake from the refrigerator, turn out on to a serving platter and spread the pineapple slices over the top. Sprinkle over a little grated nutmeg, if using. Serve immediately.

EASY　　 **SERVES 4**　　 **15 MINUTES +
4 HOURS
30 MINUTES
CHILLING**　　 **5 MINUTES**

sherry trifle

FRUIT LAYER
6 trifle sponge cakes
2 tbsp strawberry jam
6 large strawberries,
  hulled and sliced
2 bananas, peeled and
  sliced
400 g/14 oz canned
  sliced peaches, drained

6 tbsp sherry
CUSTARD LAYER
250 ml/9 fl oz double
  cream
1 tsp vanilla essence
3 egg yolks
4 tbsp caster sugar

TOPPING
300 ml/10 fl oz double
  cream
2 tbsp caster sugar
toasted, chopped mixed
  nuts, to decorate

To make the fruit layer, spread the sponge cakes with jam, cut into bite-sized pieces and arrange in the bottom of a glass serving bowl. Scatter over the fruit, pour over the sherry and reserve.

To make the custard, put the cream and vanilla essence into a saucepan and bring almost to the boil over a low heat. Meanwhile, put the egg yolks and sugar into a basin and whisk together well. Remove the cream from the heat and gradually stir into the egg mixture. Return the mixture to the pan and warm over a low heat, stirring, until thickened. Remove the custard from the heat and leave to cool for 30 minutes, then pour it evenly over the fruit layer. Cover with clingfilm and chill for 2½ hours.

Remove the trifle from the refrigerator. To make the topping, whip together the cream and sugar, then spread it evenly over the custard layer. Scatter over the toasted, chopped mixed nuts, then cover again with clingfilm and chill for a further 1½ hours. Serve chilled.

EASY  **SERVES 8 – 10** **1 HOUR 20 MINUTES** **1 HOUR**

chocolate & raspberry pavlova

4 egg whites
225 g/8 oz caster sugar
1 tsp cornflour
1 tsp white wine vinegar
1 tsp vanilla extract

300 ml/10 fl oz double
  cream, 1 tbsp caster
  sugar, 2 tbsp framboise
  liqueur, 175 g/6 oz
  fresh raspberries, and
  55 g/2 oz dark chocolate,
  shaved, to serve

Preheat the oven to 150°C/300°F/Gas 2. In a large mixing bowl, whisk the egg whites until stiff and gradually whisk in 115 g/4 oz of the sugar. In a separate bowl, mix the remaining sugar with the cornflour and then whisk it into the egg white mixture; it should be very shiny and firm.

Quickly fold the vinegar and vanilla extract into the egg white mixture.

Pile the meringue on to the baking paper with a 25 cm/ 10 inch circle drawn on the underside on a baking tray and spread evenly to the edge of the circle; swirl it around on top to make an attractive shape. Bake in the centre of the preheated oven for 1 hour.

Remove from the oven, cool slightly then peel off the paper. Place the pavlova on a large serving plate. It will shrink and crack but do not worry about this. It will keep in an airtight container for up to 2 days.

One hour before serving, whip together the cream, sugar and liqueur until thick and floppy. Pile on top of the pavlova and decorate with fruit and shaved chocolate. Chill before serving.

 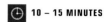

zabaglione

4 egg yolks
2 tbsp caster sugar
125 ml/4 fl oz Marsala wine
8 sponge fingers, to serve

Whisk the egg yolks and sugar together in a large, heatproof mixing bowl until light and creamy.

Place the bowl over a saucepan of hot water over a low heat and continue to whisk until the mixture begins to thicken. Gradually add the Marsala, and continue whisking until the mixture is very thick and frothy and increased in volume. Take care not to overcook it on the base of the bowl.

Remove from the stove and lift the bowl off the saucepan. Pour into individual serving dishes and serve warm or cold with sponge fingers.

quick chocolate mousse

300 ml/10 fl oz single
 cream
200 g/7 oz continental
 dark chocolate (should
 have at least 52% cocoa
 solids), such as Meunier

2 eggs, lightly beaten
2 tbsp Marsala
2 tbsp grated white
 chocolate, to decorate

Heat the cream in a saucepan over a low heat for about 3–4 minutes until almost boiling.

Break up or chop the chocolate into small pieces and place in a blender.

Pour the hot cream into the blender and then blend together until smooth.

Pour in the eggs and blend again until well mixed. Add the Marsala and give the mixture a final blend.

Pour into 6 ramekin dishes and allow to cool. Cover with clingfilm and chill for about 2 hours. Serve decorated with the grated white chocolate.

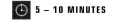
banana splits

4 bananas
VANILLA ICE CREAM
300 ml/10 fl oz milk
1 tsp vanilla essence
3 egg yolks
100 g/3½ oz caster
  sugar

300 ml/10 fl oz double
  cream, whipped
CHOCOLATE RUM SAUCE
125 g/4½ oz plain
  chocolate, broken into
  small pieces
2½ tbsp butter

6 tbsp water
1 tbsp rum
6 tbsp chopped mixed
  nuts, to decorate

To make the ice cream, heat the milk and vanilla essence in a saucepan until almost boiling. In a bowl, beat together the egg yolks and sugar. Remove the milk from the heat and stir a little into the egg mixture. Transfer the mixture to the pan. Stir over a low heat until thick. Do not boil. Remove from the heat. Cool for 30 minutes, fold in the cream, cover with clingfilm and chill for 1 hour. Transfer into an ice cream maker and process for 15 minutes. Alternatively, transfer into a freezerproof container and freeze for 1 hour, then place in a bowl and beat to break up the ice crystals. Put back in the container and freeze for 30 minutes. Repeat twice more, freezing for 30 minutes and whisking each time.

To make the sauce, melt the chocolate, butter and water together in a saucepan, stirring. Remove from the heat and stir in the rum. Peel the bananas, slice lengthways and arrange on 4 serving dishes. Top with ice cream and nuts and serve with the sauce.

index